DOWN IN THE WHITE OF THE TREE: SPIRITUAL POEMS

Tim J. Myers

Regal House Publishing

Published by
Regal House Publishing, LLC
Raleigh 27612
All rights reserved

Printed in the United States of America

ISBN -13 (paperback): 978-1-947548-47-3
ISBN -13 (hardcover): 978-1-947548-58-9
ISBN -13 (epub): 978-1-947548-48-0
Library of Congress Control Number: 2018950879

Interior design by Lafayette & Greene
Cover design by Lafayette & Greene
lafayetteandgreene.com
Cover art: "Forest Going to Seed" by Tim J. Myers

Regal House Publishing, LLC
https://regalhousepublishing.com

"...it is as if things stood with *their backs to* [us], *their faces turned to God.*"
—Abraham Herschel

CONTENTS

"At the summit of being all see and know the principle of the One."

- Kong Qiu (Confucius)

Introduction

MYSELF AS TREE: A PRAYER

Adonai,
give me life then kill me if You must,

only let it be
that like a tree I live, a planted thing,
knowing the ground deep and deeper,
drinking up world through roots I send down,
water-life drawn from soil and darkness—

let the season-round ring by ring increase me—

when sun comes, let my leaves flutter
each with its small luster—

let autumn-release fling my numberless seeds
outward on winds
shifting and sure as Hope—

and when my sap fails at last, come Thou, Axeman,
fell me hard, lay me down,
(I'll murmur Your name all the while),

stand over me gripping the ax of Death
and split me with Your hands
(the right I call Making, the left Unmaking),

Down in the White of the Tree

let the blade bite, let it jump into
my drying white interior,
oh Unspeakable, shape me, plane me—

make me a Door.

TIM J. MYERS

FEBRUARY, 1991

Tonight on the car radio
I heard a trumpet revealing,
in minor scales, the eventual death
of the sun.

At the game today a misthrown ball
went flying into the stands.
A father threw his arms around
his little girl, instantly, thoughtlessly.
The bitterness of wasted deaths
cannot overcome the truth
of his gesture.

There's a war on now. They made
love at midnight
in utter joy and abandon.
How many millennia did it take
before we could make a rake—a fence—a school?

I have books, and the great dead
as if voices in my own ears, tonight.

We must adjust the budget
for unexpected military expenditures.
In my love's belly the bones
of our child are forming.

What should I say to the
bright-specked wheeling night sky?

PALEOLITHIC BURIAL

When he died they hunched him up
like baby in womb, curled him
into a shallow scoop in the cave-floor,
planted him like a seed as he slowly stiffened,
covering his slumped and earthen limbs
with a layer of red ochre,
sprinkling him with wildflowers—
then turned away.

Moon comes back each month, so bright,
then curls itself into a dying crescent—
baby struggles out of a woman's darkness—
petals of delicate blue, pale yellow, in the wet woods,
how do they know
when sun is past dying and comes
to life again?

This is older than cities or books,
older than prayers or earnest discussions,
older than farming,
something buried and burst open long before
words, ideas, church or temple or crudest holy place,
older even than itself,

this longing.

ON LAUGHTER

Philosophers, tell us what
laughter is.

Explain this violent extraverbal utterance
leaping up through us and out,
sweetly infectious—

explain our temporary scorn
for all limits, all suffering,
for death itself, when we inhabit
the little kingdom of a joke—

explain the whole of Spring
arriving in sudden gust,
epiphany of the belly—

pore over your books,
weigh the various factors,
construct even more profound explanations
than those you've already given,
which are, I'm forced to say,
inadequate—

We've stolen the Elixir
from under your noses.

SECRETS

In summer, say,
a row of potted plants
on a sidewalk, or
trains taking people to work.
Secrets up out of
ordinary things—

how they press themselves
against all that
contains them,
these secrets,
revenants striving against
matter. Existence
as it gives life leaves so much
buried.

Set the table
carefully—you are
establishing something.
Deep-rooted willow tree.
Empty ball field.

TIM J. MYERS

AFTER PRAYER

Across from
the smoothie stand,
hummingbird in
mating dance
hovering at fifty feet
falls, light-shot
streak chittering
ecstasy.

I keep
begging God
for a sign—
World sings back, relentless,

*what greater sign
than Me?*

AT THE EDGE

At the edge of the cemetery,
where row on fetid row of the empty distorted forms
lie blank and dissolving in long boxes,
backward seeds buried in dark earth,

at cemetery-edge she leans over them
as lover might lean over beloved in desire,
a tulip tree newly flowering,
headless goddess strewing unspeakable perfections,
the deep bruise-purple and pink-white of her blossoms,
heedless of all she stands, mute, fierce,
lovely beyond telling

black trunk and black uplifted multitudinous arms,
dancer to the music of nothingness
in blind ecstasy flinging so much over the grimed carved stones

and neither the dead nor the living see her,
though she showers down her gifts with a profligacy of love,
neither the dead nor the living—though from time to time
someone glances over while hurrying past.

TIM J. MYERS

FAITH IN THE NEW WORLD

Savage men came in ships, the story says,
out of the eastern ocean, and became
the hurricane that grew stronger over land, not weaker,
never stopped coming,
a hive of pale and angry bees
hurled from darkness into the center of the world.

We could no longer honor the festival of dead children,
or of dead adults, or of warriors
in the fourteenth month when the sun walks north.
The savages came from a land of power and suffering,
cursed by plagues and strange beliefs,
hungry for odd things.
They said, *All will be judged.*
We said, *The gods are very angry.*
For a long time the whole world
was an altar for killing.
The ways of doing things fell aside
and jungle grew over them.

But the people were simple, always the same,
having made of death a dear godmother.
Holy Mother, they say, *Speak for us to your Son
in Mictlan, among the dead.
Tlaloc, bring your rain
for the baptism of our dear daughter.*
And now they sit talking and singing beside
the altar for Tia Pilar, who has died.

9

The people are like termites,
make faith out of dirt with their own hands,
press palm to palm and look to the sky,
dig up what's buried in the jungle.
Tonight they laugh,
knowing Pilar can smell the oranges and salchichas—
Oh she loved salchichas!—
knowing too
that once the hunger of ghosts is eased
with the smell of the food,

they the living will eat and be satisfied.

TIM J. MYERS

A DANCE FOR THE *DIA*

Yellow flowers of *Dia de los Muertos*—
marigold light of the sun
guides the soul back to earth—
and oh, soul of my grandfather Raoul,
we will spell your name in cloves stuck on oranges,
get you drunk on our prayers and then
listen to your stories running through our own mouths,
feel life like mariachi glow in our bodies
(having come by those bodies through you,
like clothes from a second-hand store),

and we can see you dancing,
unshaven and cackling,
when wind comes spinning paper cups over the plaza.
Grandfather! They've strung
forty-watt bulbs in a loop across the church front,
and it's your smile there,
the children are saying.

11

ADMONISHED

When I grow dark
with fear or fear of emptiness,
and looking over the world,
weak and presumptuous,
see only barren ground, worn trees,
joyless figures:

Who-Does-Not-Speak—
does not;
but as a mother, easily and smiles,

chides me with the sudden sunlit rain.

LECTURE ENGAGEMENT

He is a modern writer, has flown
across the country all expenses paid
to read his work and speak to his disciples
at our university. He rents
a car at the airport for the drive.

He can spin you ironic tales,
can sing with perfect notes of haunted schizophrenics,
chronicle the despair of housewives and intellectuals,
can lay before you war and political insanity—
he is brilliant in his depictions

of the crisis of our times.
But—(now he turns onto a little road
running along some orchards to the campus)—

concerning the apples on their branches in the dusk
and the thirty bones in each of his hands

he has nothing to say.

SACRED RIDDLE

Lost in the
desert,

that mirage
you see

isn't a sign
of flowing
spring

but of your own
thirst.

But your own
thirst—

what is it
a sign of?

LOVE-MAKING SONG

When she makes love with me
we plunge headlong far deeper than Are,
grow vaster than Will Be,
like a thrush I could pour the note-stream
out of my chest, swaying
on the thin branch of this brief life—
we are too wild-warm, too dazzle-dazed
to hold as worthy anything but our fused fury,
in Singularity scorn mere supernovae,
pretty little matchheads—
joy this joy this joy,
the sky astounds me by stubbornly remaining,
sluggish matter though blue it cannot
follow us as we rock and moan toward
whatever incandescence, shedding
useless metaphors in our wake
as easily as
worlds

AFTER A THERAVADAN SERMON

Yearning is master,
I its slave—
yearning is yearning
for the grave,

and yet I want you
willingly,
I let love have its way
with me,

my bones just kindling
for desire,
forest waiting
for its fire

but there's something
tingling there
along the roots
and through the air—

a doubleness to
desire's doom:
I phoenix as
I am consumed

SONG FOR DUST

the utterly perfect
movement of dust motes

in a column of sunlight
pouring into

the abandoned car in which
he was living,

their ease of motion,
precise unhurried
pace, as they

floated on brilliant
air—
this gave him
a measure of peace.

QUESTION PUT TO SELF

Half-rotten, crime-haunted times like these
will sure as hell teach one thing:
deep distrust of every passion
for good.

Dukkha stalks the world,
suffering is rain that falls,
not only for war-broken soldier or homeless or sick
but eating deep into Mother, Father, the kids.
My life is comfortable, my passions idealistic—
have I really faced the truth of things?
I ask myself again and again.

It's strange,
in an age hurt so badly that
it hides its head as if to ward off another blow—
in such an age to find myself
so often joyous.

So I tutor my heart with sternness,
lash it to the truth,
set gall beside its meals—

selfish intractable animal!
Still it goes burrowing toward light.

TIM J. MYERS

APRIL 2006

A famous columnist writes with disdain
of current interest in the subject of joy,
quoting strong thinkers who say it's a sign
that one isn't paying attention, a ploy

to justify self-centered ignorance,
to bury one's head in the sand,
a refusal to face the suffering of others—
and it can be this—I've seen how it can—

and yet I'm wondering, as the stink of war
keeps drifting over our airwaves, how
so many would feel such interest in such
an irrelevancy just now.

Perhaps if I were other than human,
my habits would be all right:
cat under quarter-moon happy in alleyway,
bat sweeping joyous at night.

KEEP IN MIND

Keep in mind, she said,
that in gray mid-winter
when streets are thick with road-salt and slush
and slow clocks tick dull February out,
dreams aren't dead—
wise and sluggish bears, they've merely
stumbled to their dens—
bare broadleafs only
empty for a while.

GRACE ON A MARCH MORNING

When I woke I was still in the grip
of an ugly dream, mushroom clouds
sprouting north and south—

terrified and half-asleep
I lay for a moment not thinking,
slowly realized how warm
the blankets were.

And then a bird
from its papery ribcage let out
a tangle of music, it was as if
sound became fragrance, became pouring water,

and there in the ease of first light
like a worn string I slowly
unknotted

NAMES OF GOD

For centuries Your names were kept apart,
never touching each other, divided at first
by desert or mountains or wind-swept breadth of sea,
or simply by many miles, or by the otherness
of other peoples. Each tribe had its own,
its one or its many, names made sacred to uttermost,
kept polished by intimate use
like stones rubbed for worry or luck.
Father to son, mother to daughter, each tribe
lived apart, hoarding its holy names.

But we've grown beyond our tribes,
a planetary people now, whether we know it or not—
wondering, in our cities, where the old village
has gone, the ash tree by the hut, that little bay
where we caught so many fish long ago,
the rivers and mountains and dancing grounds
of humanity's weathered past.

We dream these simple places at night,
slowly forgetting them, then dream the new places
in which our lives are now unwinding.
And the old divinities—
the ti or tikis or lares,
the Sidhe, the jinn, the venner—we look around,
Was that a—? That flash in the bushes? No.
And so must mourn the extinction of so many
spiritual fauna—

22

But Your names are flowing into a common water,
a sea. We learn other lives,
hear suddenly the music of their words for You,
tell them *We too have a great Name!*
I strain to hear them,
sweetness in each, abyss in each,
the way each did its work in human hearts.
Sometimes I think I may even have begun

to hear the One Name, the unimagined
sound

OMPHALOS

They were right, every people and tribe, when they said,
It is here, it is here—our land—
this country of ours is the heart of the world.
Here the Maker first filled His hands with dirt,
Her cupped hands with water,
and Made.
You can sense it on the air.
Something in this land goes down like roots
to the dark all-holy start of Earth.
Right here it was—look around you!,
chanting it generation to generation:
Our land is the Center of the world.

They were right, every people and tribe.

TWILIGHT PRAYER

Let the glowing pale-orange of this Colorado sunset
fade from white clouds piled
twenty-thousand feet above the blue-white Peak.

Let the aching joy in my heart fade too,
following these dulling rose-orange ramparts of cloud,
their luminous citrus-yellow edges,
as darkness exhales itself into the world.

Let each moment fade in its turn,
each life in its turn,
day and night following each other
like dancers infinitely renewed
in mutual pursuit.

This world is not just
pieces—a piece born, alive,
a piece dying, another piece.

No.

AFTER THE DINNER PARTY

She saw that
the ex-fighter pilot
is really in love
with his neighbor's wife,
and vice-versa—

tells me, *They think
nobody knows*—
and I,
having learned this from her,
know one thing
further:

that even in
his new love's arms
he will not find
what he so blindly
seeks

MASTER

We'd live our lives like cattle grazing,
lost in bovine trance—
but then the Dark One rises
and teaches us to dance.

Death cures our native deafness
with his bitter blood-wild roar—
and then we realize our hearts
have always whispered, *More...*

And so he lights our souls for us,
costumed as Disaster—
strikes up our deeper music—
becomes our dancing master.

DEATH SONG (2)

when I die
I want to feel
what mockingbird does
silent in
first starlight
at the end
of a song-crowded day

IRRATIONAL HYMN

Irreason, visit me,
discarnate because unable
with power of mind to grasp
the carnal fire within me.
Fire, burst out and rage
on the dry wood of disbelief and abstraction,
burst out, become
the unconsuming sacred fire Irreason.

Irreason, nameless, You—
nameless name of God—
and I with my small self am lacking.
Perhaps the particular I is aloof
precisely because I have a name—
but that name was my destiny,
the destiny You gave me. Come,
sink Your joy into my destiny
like man into woman, nameless in Your surge.

Irreason, sometimes You have
the features of a beast, or a sky.
I see in waking dream a stone wall
and werewolves there, in twos and threes, waiting,
standing on hind legs, leaning against the wall,
some with arms crossed, all strangely human,
waiting there in a forest clearing, waiting,
wailing a little perhaps for ghastly boredom—and You,
white strange high circle, driving all the scene.

Irreason, the reason in me springs from You
as water from a cleft of stone comes spilling.
Irreason, You've sprinkled lambs like snow
over the green fields, and will sprinkle snow.
Irreason, You pulse in my lover's face.

Irreason, You aim me endlessly at song.
Irreason, driver of planets, trembler of sound,
eye-bright of color, quintessence, oh Irreason!

Perhaps it is that, being part of You,
I must become Your mystery, which I am—
in all my forms, in every step of my fate,
perform that single most difficult task: to simply
and in all mind-twisting, death-haunted profundity
be. To be, Irreason. One thing I know:
that I was born to You, unanswering One,
source of every answer, adored Irreason.

JUNK WINDCHIMES

When I clean the garage I find myself
thinking about it without a word in my head:
decay.
I hold in my hands the fate of things;
it comes up like a smell.
The stroller crippled with use, diseased
by the baby's continual health;
dusty bottles like wombs gone barren, holding nothing;
crumbling newsprint to say only
that said becomes unsaid,
and somewhere in the back of my mind I'm remembering
how flesh is only a firmer kind of cardboard.

The windchimes lay tangled on a stack of tiles,
a tasteless organization of bronze and tin
in the shape of an owl,
big-eyed cute like on a Hallmark card,
tiny bars dangling.
Why did I spend that quarter hour
unraveling rusted strips and strings?
Finally I held them up and gave
a little wind-like shake—

Oh infinity! Shimmering rain on the driveway weeds!
It is the life in the vessels, not the vessels—
chiming came whole and pure as souls from the fire.

IN MARCH

A couple on Brinkerhoff Street
are fighting, car door to back door,
he slams his contemptuously as she yells
"...never put anything fucking away...
Heaven fucking forbid!"—

while along their chain-link fence,
crocuses have announced in white silence
those sentences of which Spring itself
is the Unspeakable,
low petals so anciently pure,
beggars beatified at roadside,

and coming down the sidewalk
a saint in jeans and an old jacket
can hardly distinguish the two,
the fight from the crocuses,
looking on them from some distant stupid joy
he'd have to travel a million miles
to emerge from.

BEFORE AN ANCIENT BAS-RELIEF

As dawn sun fell full
on the carved wall,
half-ruined and overgrown as it was
in that wild place—

with no one else near,
I reached out thinking to touch
their lost bright centuries,
their knowledge—

but standing there, fingertips
against a carved stone face,
felt the Light

rushing up out of my own darkness,
welling up through my arm,
to meet Itself

there in the chiseled stone.

HE GLIMPSES THE BREADTH OF LOVE

We love each other, saying that as if
our love were something *in* us, or *between* us.
No: Around us,
breathing our two names in and out of
its vast mysterious lungs—

around us like a forest at night,
a planetary atmosphere known only
one small breath at a time,

fruit at whose center little seeds sleep,
thinking they know.

TIM J. MYERS

FOR EDGAR ALLAN POE

I have absolutely no pleasure in the stimulants that I sometimes so madly indulge. It has not been in the pursuit of pleasure that I have periled life and reputation and reason. It has been in the desperate attempt to escape from the torturing memories, from a sense of some insupportable loneliness, and a dread of some impending doom.

—Poe

I make this song for him, pray this prayer:
That Poe, whose body lay
in filthy clothes on some county examiner's table,
empty as a fish on a slab,
ascended—ascends—and in sudden
paroxysm sloughs off like dead skin
his dread—(suffering, in that bright
unknown place, falling from him like
a rain)--and then with a wrenching unutterable
sweetness of absolute orgasm wakes
shuddering from extinction to the always-gaze
of mother's father's lover's eyes, that in
tenderness and infinite passion,
wordlessly, worldlessly,

love him.

X-RAY

In a heartsore time I prayed for signs,
relentlessly teleological, grim in my pursuit
of solace, hunger-driven, fear-driven,
desolate in self-absorption—

found myself one day at the hospital
after jamming my thumb playing ball—
and afterwards, the white-haired lady said,
It's all digital now. Want to see them?

So I looked, my spirit half-asleep, hung over
on the mescal of nauseous fear:
that familiar white on black—
but suddenly I
saw:

calcium cosmos-shaped to loveliness—
temple columns of purest moon-white—
pale joyous slaves, fluted, mouthless,
singing their sutras, shuras, glorias—

heard, from beneath
the surface of the world my skin,
archangel voices from those bone-ghosts in my hand:

*You are the ones assigned
to look for answers—we only
sing—*

THE DISCOVERY OF EXTRASOLAR PLANETS, 1990'S

Between the lines of terse newspaper accounts,
I hear these oceans so many light-years away,
see trees I wouldn't recognize as trees,
strain to glimpse across the gulfs
an animal moving through strange underbrush,
houses, music, those who sing whatever songs.

I can wring such marvels from dry astronomical reports,
stellar rotational blips, gas giants at seventy light-years—
it's easy! I'm human, a storytelling animal,
can sense beyond careful telemetric numbers
fiction slowly giving way to fact.

Spirit, beat me numb with the great emptiness
and still I'll dream—
still the ghost-quasar of possibility
will electrify the star-fields
in my little head!

SONG FOR THE INTIMATIONS

A man or woman amid groves in springtime
but will sometimes be lonelier than if they stood
on vast frozen prairies in deepest February,
skeletons to shrieking wind and obliterate storm.
And why?
Because it's the intimations
that drive us crazy,
hurl us toward exultation or the nameless grief.

It's the same reason that humans,
burning with *should be*,
so easily forget joy,
know sorrow page by page, like a book,

while the bears, the crows, the burrowing mice
are always forgetting it

(unless, of course, they breathe
some stupendous secret
far beyond such things)

TIM J. MYERS

MARCH NIGHT

There is such peace in the night sky,
such ease of planets and numberless stars,
such tranquil infinite volumes,
that all my yearning hovers and rests.
There is such sleep; night after night
a dark washing and soothing,
a healing each dawn completes.

This peace torments more than all my fears.
It drives me—after soothing me—to seek
and find its source, this cool dream
of the universe, this nameless peace.

TRANSPHYSICAL SONG

Gathering and releasing what I am,
and you are all I've ever seen,
Love suddenly visits our bodies,
possesses them wholly:

Suddenly
we're blue-green wavecrest
sensing the slope of beach,
stands, arcs perfectly, curls,
shudders to milk-white foam—

Suddenly
we're hard winter ground
just cusping under warm winds,
a March night, up through wet earth
numberless green shoots pressing—

Suddenly
we're two red-tailed hawks
high on a cold wind,
wheeling without strokes
three thousand feet past wondering about

the spent bodies of two lovers
on grass far below, motionless,
still touching

HYMN TO PEREGRINE MUTABILITY

It's the hamster we bought our sons
all those years ago—I keep thinking about it,
furry little escape artist, endlessly gnawing
at the bars of the cage, the plastic water dish,
pushing at corners, squeezing itself into any cranny—
and of course it got out—
I'd be watching TV after everyone was in bed,
catch a flash of furred motion along the living-room floor,
my brain screaming *Rat!*—then breathe again,
only Gilly on the lam like before.
I'd gather her up—she never got far.

Night after night, like a prison movie
about desperate men living only
for the break—and the noise as she
chewed and pushed and prodded away,
not understanding the strength of metal,
not understanding the confusing layout of our apartment,
not understanding this was no longer
the Syrian desert from which her ancestors were taken
(and promptly escaped back into, some of them—
scientists having underestimated
their drive to be free, fierce rodent determination).
We've "domesticated" hamsters—
meaning in this case that
if we toss them into small steel jails
there's a chance they'll actually stay put.
We build them little cities of plastic tubing,

believe they're happy, are getting used to it. Still,
all night long they're sniffing, poking, testing,
rattling, picking, straining,

and when she died, my little sons heartbroken
to find her still on the cage floor
(a stillness wholly unlike the only half-settled stillness
of her sleep among the cedar shavings)—

when I realized she was dead
I instantly thought, *Escape!*—or *Escape?* (in that
fundamental human sacrament we call Doubt).

This isn't just a matter of hamsters, of course.
Look around.
"Nothing lives forever but rocks and sky,"
the Cheyenne say—but sorry, guys,
we've got astronomy, cyclotrons, the Hubble telescope:
Nothing lives forever. Period.
Space-time itself is meta-wired
for demise, sudden death or gradual dissipate death,
even the stars, those ancient juggernaut lamps,
are churning their own nuclear guts out at fixed rates,
conjuring hydrogen to helium, measuring out
their gargantuan lives in something analogous to coffee spoons.
And someday, WHAM!—supernova. Or else
emptying and cooling to dwarf-cinder,
running its withered course like
any grape left on the vine.

But it's not just
extinction.
And this understanding has come to me slowly,

stirring me to my depths, as if
someone I can't see keeps tapping me on the shoulder,
has something to say I haven't yet heard.
Visions of universal entropy and decay, yes,
but something more at the heart of it,
something far vaster than what I've known, far deeper—
not salt to corrode the hull of my ship of self—
not salt, but mysterious salt waves upholding.

I think again of our hamster,
of the Big Bang, that single Root differentiating itself
into all of life and death. Everything is
going some place, going some place,
it's like one of those old black-and-white movies
where Saturday-afternoon hero in a boat
is heading for the waterfall—

only it's everything, quarks, atoms, molecules, elements,
inanimate, animate, planets, stars, galaxies, the whole
blazing dark empty light-strewn place itself—
no line of marching ants more determined
than this, more directed, I ache with the failure
of my attempts at extrapolation,

what does that cataract at the edge of existence
empty into?

Day by day, my hamster-fierce
curiosity, the soul-hunger I can never fill
with mere feed-pellets and sunflower seeds,
day after day, night after night I'm
hammering out a rhythm as I test the bars,
gnawing at, singing at the Question that always scorches

DOWN IN THE WHITE OF THE TREE

my little mammalian soul:

Why should Everything be
such a relentless Traveler?

AS WE HIKED

"This is as far as we go," he said.
We were hiking the Rampart Range
through pinyon pine and one-seed juniper,
summer storm hanging just south of us
over the Peak. The talk had turned
metaphysical.

"As far as we go," he insisted,
grinding his boot in the dust of the trail,
a little ritual about
extinction.

we go, we go, sang the dust,
dust that leaps up into breathing shapes,
wondering, rueful, singing dust,
pounded by time into pounding heartbeats

THE ANGEL THANATAEL

He bends over the dying
as mother or father would, tenderly,
over sleeping child,
bends to us and calls us away.

Comes with a kind of joy no human can recognize,
with a pry bar to pry free, gently, the clinging animus.
Watches as souls slip off
like octopi to deeper waters
from shallow bays beneath the summer moon.

To the deathly ill, his face at bedside means
an end to the lava-flow of unremitting pain,
the stupor induced by profound medicines.
To the weary he is at last
the Johnny Appleseed their bones have waited for,
longing to be planted, to bear
some other kind of blossom.

He sees the horror in our faces,
we're aghast at his sudden presence,
he knows we can't see who he really is.

For he offers more love, suffers more compassion,
discharges more tenderly his appointed duties
than any among the celestial host,
Michael, Gabriel, Raphael
cold and roughshod by comparison.

46

TIM J. MYERS

Has no one understood
that he stands just there,
at the right hand of the Throne?

SONG FOR FIVE O'CLOCK

Just after five, as the working day
goes flat like a punctured tire,
a man and woman in an unwashed sedan
are together in the sense
that two ragged chunks of concrete
dumped by the river are together,
and he drives with all the absent concentration
of having followed the same streets way too many times,
and she drags on a cigarette, setting
an already hard face a little harder—
to what consternation I have no idea—
and they can't be more than twenty-five, either of them.
Just then the winter sun
frees itself of smudging high stratus
for the first time today,
breaks in on them, gold, with a driving pure light
even an Old Master couldn't have mixed,
had he God's own palette. Gold
on the dirty cars, dusty streets. But
nothing in their emptiness stirs at this,
or wonders, or notices, nothing
deters them from this drive home
in evening traffic. I see all this
in ten, maybe fifteen seconds, as they
press vacuously on through the intersection.

ORANGE

as the green of young oranges
(half-lost amid the jade-dark of many leaves)
with such infinite mindless patience
through the winter months
silently turns
orange—

a color at first
only hinted at,
only dreamed of by the sweetening fruit,
but with sunlight's sexual insistence
swelling day by day toward
something—

and now, as time seems to fold on itself
in the sex-act of deep season,
spring comes, that orange so utter, so powered that
it glows noon or twilight,
is like a great sound against the leaves,
orangeness made
music—

just this way, after
a hard winter
of doubt and fear,
my faith comes
back

TO THE FLOWERS OF THE CREPE MYRTLE

As I would praise a great hero, I praise you:
mute, but your blossoms red-pink
to an intensity beyond my tears at seeing them,

as if a century of world had flowed
into a single petal;
as if a boy could see far into time
his wife, his children;
as if the Nameless One should come
and stand before me.

And deep, here, down in me
where my own will can never reach,
waiting for eons in profound sleep
while body's sleep and wakefulness
ebbed and flowed so high above,
I was only a silence

till you eased my true eyes open
and at last I

woke

WE MODERNS

We all keep wailing about death, death!,
Bertrand and his descendants assure us
the whole thing's just one gigantic fuck-up,
and if some bumpkin says
we can find peace somehow,
or if the Miracles come on the oldies station
singing *It's all right...*
and for a second or two the "tough-minded"
let down their guard, feel something warm and strange—
well then, that's just
weakness, sentiment, an emotional
anomaly. Because they'll soon
remember themselves and suck it up,
bend again to the fashioning of elegant despair.

And why?
Because we've
submitted—

have refused to dream
of the heat we can't imagine
at the hearts of stars.

HER HUSBAND'S DEATH

Grief, do you see
how you've mourned me dry,
how only the many years
can do my work of forgetting now?

Because that's all I really have
to fight you with: forgetting.
My indignation rises—
but after wild anguish grows
quiet. Hope is there only like
the repeated flickerings of spring
throughout geologic time.

The work, beneath my heart,
is to take up life's rhythm again
in spite of the images hollowing my sleep—
his face, his eyes—

The work goes on.
I can feel it even beneath the agony,
I know something, but too far down
to cherish or be eased by.
Someday I'll remember
that this enforced forgetting,
this attempt to lie to myself in the face of loss,
is only for a while,

Tim J. Myers

I'll remember that he
will hold me again in that world
beyond days and numbers,

when you, Grief
(good creature though I hate you,
doing what you're meant to do),
when even you have

finally unwound and
come undone, like the smoke of a world
passing into   .

LIBERATION SONG

Waiting for an early bus,
dull with sleep and the weight of myself, my problems,

I heard a flurry of small wings,
turned and saw

two sparrows struggling in the lock of love
on thick grass under a tulip tree,

just then a sudden wind
shook loose three white petals

Tim J. Myers

THOSE ROSES

Those roses I gave you, their scarlet eagerness spent,
stood in the vase withered and defeated,
and I was surprised, oddly so, of course,
having known long since that they'd die—

so what did I expect? Like a kindergartener
at his grandpa's funeral I stood vacant,
surprised to remember that everything disappears.
Passion has befuddled me—

or whispers something deeper:

that no symbol of this love we've found,
this great thing, this sky, reverberant union,
no symbol can outlast the thing itself, or overreach
its beauty--not these roses, or these words, not even

these bodies, yours and mine, our lips and eyes,
which though they burn can only symbolize.

AFTER BERNINI'S *ECSTASY OF ST. THERESA*

Hewn to a native weakness by the powers
of earth that gave me being, by the Hands
within the handlessness of biological
process, of bursting incandescent original egg,
I see what I am and know: Myself am sin.

Original or otherwise, willed
or otherwise, I am—and all like me are—
half-desolate in this, that being finite
we must stand apart, sing separate,
every action partialed by its loneliness.

But You—You!—oh surge and take me,
dry wild driftwood dreaming of Your fire—
a woman's ache her empty place to fill—
this mind's half-ghosted thoughts imparadised
by wholly You—word-skimmed, hyacinth-Real!

TIM J. MYERS

TWO POEMS FOR TRUTH

1.
Having noticed by now that truth is elusive,
a skein, a breath, but powerful to the heights of heaven,
a kind of food for us, appearing and disappearing
on our plates—

having noticed these things I see Anubis—
the scales, weighing out a death—
the feather which is truth, airy thing,
that a breeze would spin crazily in the air
(if air ever entered that soundless chamber)—

and Osiris, green-skinned and wise,
looking down at the scales where
the dead man's heart, blood-gorged
weighty lump, sluggish straining organ, tries
to balance itself with truth.

2.
Like a dog I am and truth my master,
whose blows I endure heartsick,
whose hands on my neck and chest I love,
but either way my master, and I must follow.

And when he sets me loose on open ground,
to run with all my strength in cold bright air!

ON JANUARY 6TH

I called out
in grief and
the silence of
an empty world,
Lord!—

Through graylight winter air
heard, felt nothing,
went gray with gray
hunger, mute
whine of it
inside me,

until, gaunt in that
bony January wind,
I suddenly heard Him
there and quiet in

my own voice

TIM J. MYERS

CAPITOLA BEACH, NEW YEAR'S DAY '03

On the day traditionally set aside
for taking stock and recovery from drinking
(not hard to see the connection there),

we walked the flat shell-strewn beach
in easy winter sunlight with that
summery Californian intimation of paradise.
Barefoot amid sparkling rivulets and foam-wash,
we laughed and talked, till one of our sons
(soon to graduate college, the other already on his own)

called to us from tumbled rocks near the cliffside, pointing.
We crossed to him—gasped. There in paler rock
within a dark boulder, but clear even to
the tiny porousness of bone:
a fossil vertebra bigger than my hand:
whale.

We soon found more:
a chain of smaller vertebrae, spine-pieces
diminishing along the ancient beast's tail.
Then someone stumbled on
a larger section of the long-dead back,
every inch clear as print to read in the book of the rock.
A local expert later told us
he'd never seen that fossil before,
that currents and winter surf are always churning up
new marvels on that beach,

the layers there three to five million years old.

We stood before it, hearts pounding.
I put my hand out, touched what was once
the knuckles of that sea-heaving back,
imagining how the colossal muscled torso
hung along the delicate boneline—
foolishly reached for a name to call him—
across those millions of years found only
whale

Even as we chirped like birds, happy in our discovery,
we all mourned his end, I think, in secret,

aggrieved that death had etched him into stone,
shrunk his great ocean-roaming life to this pale imprint—

but sensing more, we felt that storm-rush of wonder,
in the backward abysm catching at something,
our little minds reeling, hearts suddenly
so much bigger than they usually are...

I take the nameless whale now
as one of my saints. I have questions for him.
They rise in me like something
deep currents keep bringing back to sunlit shores.
Self by its nature cries out to know the Mystery
that left this whale here as if
some great, mute, singing ghost-bird.
The more I become myself, the more I become
a series of simple mysterious questions
hung from a backbone of passionate sacred curiosity—
and someday, of course, will myself be no more than

small bones singing *why*.
That's the birdsong of self.

And what will my own bones learn,
waiting quietly in the earth like his,
as whole ages teeter and slip away,
seas eat at new Americas,
stars flicker on and off like each spring's flowers?

SNAPDRAGON IN SPRING

Standing alone I waited,
wrapped in an eternity
of my own fragrance,
still except for shiftings of the air.

So perfect had I become,
so wrought to pitch of color
and grace of leaf, so pressed by spring
to beauty! But alone.

Inviolate chamber walls
were dusted with my need.
I waited. Coming summer
seemed a torture of perfection.

But then how sweetly came that thrust,
that fire through my pistils—
how I've longed to plunder this soul of mine!—
that thunderous buzzing, toward me, over the grasses!

A PRAYER BEFORE SEX

Into bed, you witch!
Throw back the blankets!
Give us smooth sheets,
air on our skin!
Give me your legs and belly,
give yourself, give now and wild!
Up with your dress, down with your silks!
I'm naked already, I'll press you
with all I am! Give me your breasts
in soft air warming!
Let me enter you, straining and stiff,
take me, succulent, love me,
as one great pulse of pleasure strive with me
to celebrate in shouting strength
our immortality!

LOVE SONG (2)

Summer night, our root and flower,
I have been billowed from myself
by this wind of love,
lilac fragrance tumbling from the boughs.

We touch each other, branches stirring—
alone I couldn't feel the half of this—
and love fills us like lilac scent
drifting from the window through our room.

Lilacs die when spring is full. Tonight I know,
as we lie close, that Paradise will be
something like this love, this fragrance,
and we will lie together.

TIM J. MYERS

TO FIND

to find my faith
I not only climbed mountains

but tunneled down in the dark at the roots of
mountains—

like Inanna, Orpheus, Baldur, the Hero Twins before me
made my way

to the Land of the Dead

WE THINK WE KNOW THAT COUNTRY

In this century many have become
tourists in the country of Despair.
Tourists, not inhabitants—
that's the crux of it.

We hover at the border in a gray town,
turn from bitter winds pouring off those merciless steppes,
drink and joke in well-lit inns
just this side of the line,
though our laughter and drunken joy
can never penetrate the immeasurable silence.

Some have actually crossed over,
pitched rude camps a mile or two in,
either for devotion to truth
or out of some fascination grown too immense—
or just to be in style.
They keep scrambling back like freaked-out Klondikers,
eyes blank.

Some stay right on the line,
live out their days there,
make it their livelihoods—
and talk about it? Hell, sing about it,
shout to the four winds,
publish books and essays, speeches, librettos,
most of it the same few thoughts
broken into howls. But they're only

a few steps in, you see—haven't really
gone native, as it were.

For if they'd penetrated the ashen hinterland,
been swallowed up in its crushing soundlessness,
the trance of such citizenship would preclude
the writing of books or poems
or any such vanities.

I was no tourist; hated it. Sank
from subject to worker to slave,
buffeted on the hurricane of my own blood
across endless provinces of black grass and empty burrows,
smashed toward its capital
by my own desire grown monstrous,
flung pell-mell through streets of ragged brick
in the narrow ever-night, kicking and screaming
like a rabbit picked up to be gutted.
Then felt the wind suddenly cease:

enormous quiet of ten thousand empty doorways—
full moon lighting dead fountains and plazas—
my own legs walking me against my will
into the moon-shot temple of shadows
at the city's rank center—
stood before the eidolon
of that helot nation
to which all contribute endless revenue:

saw in hulking dark stone
the headless statue of Mother with twins at her empty breasts,
worshipped her like an automaton in fever.

It was going all the way in,

losing myself forever—only then could I see
the abyssal motherhood of death,
only then stand up straight enough,
find strength enough, to loathe the place,
to spurn its narrow worship,
turn on my heels and begin
the hundred thousand miles home.
Concerning this journey, the vastness of my mother tongue
has nothing to say.

At last I saw wheeling crows and ragged tents,
knew the border was near,
sleazy cantinas and flophouses,
brothels where everyone fucks but no one touches

but by that time had discovered
another kind of
Silence.

TO KALI

I can see the null-dark of Your eyes,
hear Your crashing music as it
moves through the worlds,
numberless deaths comprise
its ever-tottering melody.
You sway in your skirt
of severed human arms.

How can so vast a dark be?
How can so vast a dark be
You?

There are vortices about Your pupils,
galaxies colliding, waters
drowning all, raging the light,
I'm a goddamn bug!

But even darkness
is You,
I see You
and my bones go jumping like salmon upstream
toward their natal headwaters,

I'll praise, if I can,
even this faceless, light-smothering, vein-opening
aspect of
Your magnificence

WHEN DEATH

When Death was my suitor, inconstant, and I waited him
as a girl soon to be woman might wait,
bitter with dread fascination
because he crooned and dallied with me,
sick to my stomach like a child ignored but then
suddenly terrified at what
he might want to do when we're alone,

in the shut house I mourned.

That is, until the winter sun broke free
(Earth pivoting somewhere on its unfathomed ellipse),
and over my snow-humped city blared a gold-gray radiance,
bringing life more bright than flowers
to my close-set window glass;

and to the suitor, lax, of whom I was shed,
I tossed my long hair in contempt,
walking out into the great light of the world,
my wild heart mended.

TIM J. MYERS

APPLE TREES IN EARLY WINTER

They stand. That's the thing of it.
Gnarled into shapes like constantine wire,
dark-boled and scraggly with
those few leaves not yet ripped away
by wind's ungainly wrath—they stand.

Here and there a single apple hangs,
the red of it forlorn in a graying world,
juice now past its sweetness. The farmer
rarely comes to the orchard now.

If only I could get the trick of this,
this standing, this silent patience.
Sadness in the winter landscape weighs
nothing to them, it seems, can't darken
their lives, whatever thoughts
in the slow deep sap they think—

See, they must have bound themselves over
in service to something deeper.

GOING TO BED IN MY PARENTS' HOUSE

Oh time-swept, quasar-beaded
Lord of Heaven and Earth,
Oh Pantocrator, violent silken One:

When I sleep, on vacation, in my parents' extra room,
let the wind come up in the deep of night,
let its roar in the neighbors' poplars wake me to joy,
let your fancy, Lord, run abroad in the world,
your night-swollen wind boom out!

NIGHT WAKING

I wake at night
to booming wind in tall trees,
moonlight leaping everywhere
through intricate leaf shadows—

as if my heart—
sacred desiring beast wanderer—
had finally gone abroad and become all things!

INCA DIG

He peers at me from a magazine cover, empty sockets,
skull and bones so old, teeth in the death-clenched jaw,
that they seem to have traveled halfway back to mud.
Finger bones clasped before him,
he still wears a brown cloak
(woven by skilled fingers now desiccated to ghostliness)
and the cloth cap of a headdress, from which,
splayed by the packed earth of his long home,
fan the still-glowing feathers of jungle birds.

Funded professors dug him up
from beneath the shantytown schoolyard of Tupac Amaru.
Peruvian soil drier than the moon
kept his bones firm in the cage-like interlockings life gave them
while time's soft hammer beat all the color out
(How many summers and winters? More than
the endless flocks of migrating birds),

while over his head a town's worth of people
are now trying to live,
refugees from guerilla war in the highlands,
cooking oil, blaring radios, dust, they are very poor,
do they feel strange kinship with
people taken out of the ground from when
Pizarro worked his ignorant brutality
across an empire? So much has gone dark—

all but these feathers on the bony head,

74

still iridescent blue,
still undying orange of the sun,
still hummingbird emerald.

This is the strange inner current always riding my pulse,
the other beat of my every heart-thump.

And this is the way I'll go to death if I can,
cockade of brilliant feathers at my temple,
a soldier armed with nothing but color and light,
chieftain of no realm of dirt and water.

They say the children of Tupac Amaru
lost a soccer ball, kicked it too far,
halfway to the sun it seems, for it sank
in a hole in the earth, a tomb
we've now dug up, door to someplace, we think,
some dead but real place,

of course I want to see too, want a glimpse
of his ancient life. But I'm distracted as
these bunched feathers say (in the only voice
bone-man has left in this world)

I was a man, but my life-joy
has eaten me elsewhere—
this body now only a spent chrysalis,
rusted signpost beside
a road

ON LANGUAGE

Language is the border of the truth.

Like the border of the Empire,
where the Emperor's fine maps end,
guards standing bored and disgruntled
at the edge of the Western provinces.
It's a little town, haunted by barbarians
who strike suddenly from the wilderness,
and by blue-gray mountains rising far away.
You approach the gates, leading a donkey
loaded with books, but the sullen gatekeeper
has no stomach for scholars.
"Dump the books, old man," he growls,
"They don't mean anything out there,
and they won't stop Bird-Immortals or barbarians.
You're a fool to leave the Empire. Why not
just put a knife to your throat and be done with it?"
But all the same he unlocks the gates,
swinging the worn posts outward, and you see
the gaunt beauty of autumn frost on those
wild blue-gray slopes in the distance—

and they are your destination.

TIM J. MYERS

FOR STEPPING OUT UNDER THE STARS

The edge of my heart, the farthest edge,
I can't see it across these depths,
too far, too far, in star-lengths unbounded,
here in my chest

SONG OF BEING

While the ontologists and epistemologists
and other athletes of reason
strive toward the architecture of their thought
(trying to stack those crazy bricks we call *words, ideas*)—
while these thinkers pursue their appointed tasks
of definition, analysis and logic,

down on the fair grounds after the festival,
as drunk people here and there are snoring under trees
and dawn comes pale over the littered midway,
some musicians are playing quietly together
a little chicano song that hops
like a bird goes hopping over the grass.

TIM J. MYERS

REMIND ME

it will remind me
of itself, the world:
there's strong wind
as I step out
into the garden—
it will remind me,
will say, Look at
this particular sky,
these light-rubbled ranges
of cloud, this
gull's wings splayed
translucent as it banks—
whispering, *Look,*
look at this—
look harder

IN PRAISE

The One who made all that is
loved the coming together of things,
and therefore scattered throughout the cosmos
an infinite zoology of cohesion:

gravity itself, the prime Gatherer;
heavy attractors; galactic centers; black holes;
planets (strange spheres where matter accretes);
islands; nodes; joints; ganglia; lovers; families; nations;
the sudden unified arrangement we call a *body*;
that social joining we term a *people*;
even that mysterious flowing of many into one that we call
self—

but also made each coming together
a falling apart,
Something and Nothing the two-faced Janus
on our great Temple door—

and then, out of some deeper thought
we can never know,
made fine that line between
cohesion
and the infinitely dissipated state we call
nothingness;

and set that line in us,
right down the middle of who we are,

80

so that, as we live,
over that raging delicate fine line

we go dancing

A NIGHT PRAYER

My little son asleep,
his face more beautiful
in nightlight glow
than I've ever seen it—

I will die, he will die, this love
for him that fills me till
I can't contain it—we will all
be parted, parted. I go

to my bed, lie beside her. Why
did we make him at all?
I ask in anguished silence, knowing
the way of things. But
she sleeps unaware. And I

roll over, smiling wryly,
my despair drained off as quickly
as it came. Disbelief is
tempting, in a half-logical way,

but for God's sake—it's all beyond us!
We wanted our boy. We made him.
There he lies, beautiful and alive.

And all the universe is bound by this.

Tim J. Myers

TO THE GHOST OF FRANCOIS VILLON

He considers it nature's unforgivable sin to ravish
us with loveliness and then dissolve it in our arms.
                    —Will Durant, *The Reformation*

Francois, these five hundred years,
rising like vast mountain ranges
between your war-broken France and my consumer America
still haven't changed the fate of men and women,
have they?

We wake to life, our bodies grow to ardor,
hearts combusting as the torch of existence is put to them,
we endlessly seek
the perfect contentment, perfect embrace—
till all burns down level again.

But you, Francois—maybe the ache
that seems never to have left you
was another kind of emptiness:
beaten, ignored, destitute,
thief and wastrel, tramp and streetfighter,
what could you have known of the roots
of happiness? If hunger and penury hadn't
snapped always at your heels like the dogs of the Quarter,
if someone had once loved you beyond all reckoning—
what would your song be then,
what ravishments might you have found
the perfect notes for?

Down in the White of the Tree

Ah, maybe even the ignorant priests
were right in their way—maybe our deaths,
our absence from this world we love
so reluctantly, so completely,
are presence unfathomed in some bliss-shot
Unsomewhere always
(the idiot Love keeps insisting it's so)

which the fragrance of this world's blossoms,
peach and apple, cherry and plum,
in their tiny strength

can only prefigure.

TIM J. MYERS

ON BECOMING

When some music runs its liquor through my veins,
suddenly takes me, takes all I am,
remakes me in its own image—
in that moment I feel what the salmon feels
first sniffing, from offshore waters,
its birth-river's beckoning mouth.

That time my young sons came running,
threw themselves into my arms,
and I felt all my love for them in the instant—
just then I knew the ache of bare March trees
for summer's crowding leaves.

The night I told Cilla I loved her,
never having said the thing before—
then I was the momentary volume
of some high mountain headwaters
five thousand miles from the sea.

Always in the blossoming of time into
a particular longed-for event,
there's that same dark sweetness
of unthinkable journeying—
our futures laid out in mysterious holiness,
still tasting of Earth's battering primal seas,
still warm with the heat of the newly cooling planet,
but darkened too with unimaginable
interstellar distances—

Down in the White of the Tree

and I feel the cry and the sleep
and the death and the sexual ecstasy of all my race,
and in my creaturehood can sense, infinitely far off,
the pulse of the one thunderous
Blood

(and I thought I was shut up in
a little room of self!)—

there at center of my depth
hear my own voice say
I am

becoming

MUSE (2)

She streeled up to my house after midnight,
one of those buxom, craggy-looking divorcees,
banged on the door till I crawled out of bed
and came down.
I didn't even know her; booze on her breath;
and she kept on about how she felt like dancing,
shaking her tail right there on my porch,
talking too loud, some oddball off the streets.
Oh, I'd seen her around.
So I'm standing there in my boxers, craving sleep,
how was I supposed to get up for work in the morning?
But she's talking a mile a minute, doing
her boozy bump-and-grind
in the cut-grass and lilac smell of suburban spring darkness—
so I said this or that, to get rid of her,
sent her off to wherever it was
she'd crash for the night,
closed the door with relief,
locked it.

But in the morning noticed
an odd looseness in my thighs;
a waking-after-love-making feel...

Some time after,
the poem began
to uncurl in darkness toward its birth.

NUMBERS

Each a stick-man stiff and dead
and yet they march together
to infinity and back,
grown small enough that their leaders
can fit on my hands.

What pretty capers these zombies cut,
if one can command them,
jinn called up with a few strokes on paper—
but then only do what they're told.
Slaves, but can net the stars.

Have visited quasars and returned
from the edge of all things
with monotonous profound reports.
And they were who they are
even before the Big Bang,
slept in some strange life prior to
primal exploding Egg.

Prime to googolplex, the more they always are,
how many? Our drones,
but we can't count them, not even
with themselves.

I speak their little names, taste
the uncanniness
of how things are.

TIM J. MYERS

ETYMOLOGICAL HYMN

In seeking the etymon, the 'true sense' of a word, the Greeks were engaging in no idle quest...
—William Umbach

In distant reaches of the past, it seems,
we still knew words as if they were real—
would crack them open to eat,
would rise or fall before their power,
would use them with greater care, long before
science, advertising, politics
began to freeze-dry utterance for their own purposes:

Bear, for instance, which translates as *brown one*,
actually a mere shadow-word for one
too sacred, too horrible to say.
Hindus and Slavs of the long-dead world, to avoid it,
called him "honey-eater," the Celts "honey-pig"—
people too awed to be presumptuous,
turning their eyes to the ground so's not to look on
the majestic, cloud-riven, storm-dark, sun-burning
Face in all things.

All ancient peoples knew this sanctity, this terror,
fled from the saying of the august
Word.
But it's not word-magic I long for,
not mumbled spells or names of gods and devils;
of course they're only sounds arbitrarily assigned.

89

Down in the White of the Tree

But how long ago did we understand
that we cannot understand?
How long since we built *Adonai's*,
temple-like euphemisms, verbal iconostases,
tetragramattons, offered such humble reverence?
Only the priests of Israel could speak God's true Name,
and then only once a year, in the Inner Temple—
and Solomon, the stories tell us,
adjured the jinn with Its blazing might.

How many centuries did it take
till we grew casual about our dictionaries,
forgetting the world's naked power, naked radiance,
forgetting the altar-consummation
of any language we put to it,
the danger and glory
of taking such flames as words into
our own little mouths?

I sense the Brown One in my dreams at night,
humped shadow huffing somewhere
off beyond the lilac hedges;
the sharp smell of Him comes to my nostrils.
He seems to wander the empty shopping mall at night.
And if in my ignorance I should someday come
face to face with Him,

what Name shall I offer?

TIM J. MYERS

FROM THE BIKE TRAIL

that instant: hawk's lean body
vehement to air offered,

hosanned in lightslant,
radiant

over weeds sunheavy and still,
where city buildings rose and fell—

acts,
contracts:

one moment tent-like spread,
all lines and corners, stretched,

but then: dark-diamond eye, swift,
catches mouse-scurry, wren-flit—

stops—stalls—
sudden falls,

become mere object, void-abandon,
empty-eyed, intent only on

prey-swoop, fear-swivel:
a plummeting chisel.

Down in the White of the Tree

Then: invisible blow—hard-struck meat—
taloned rodent, songbird beaked—

the down-arc bottoms, up-swerves over
clustered yarrow, dawn-wet clover,

then angles off to hidden branch
there to feed, and thus give back

unthinking the supernal gift
life in silence gives to it,

gift for gift, blind praise to Giver,
near the train tracks by the river.

TIM J. MYERS

LEAP OF FAITH

Looking down from where
I stand precariously
on this pinnacle
of consciousness, I see
my life always falling away from me—

plummeting headlong into
the unknown
immensity—

What else can I do
but jump after it,

all of me?

BUDDHISTS BELIEVE IN 16 KINDS OF VOIDS

So do I.

The first is at utmost center
of heron's watchful eye.

The second exists deep within
the furious failure of the twister
to stay upright, spin in place.

The third is there in a baby's brain
as soft bones in the top of its skull grow shut.

The fourth is the immensities between galaxies.

The fifth is that small emptiness
burning without consummation
at the core of a murderer's heart.

The sixth is what musicians call
a rest—
silence flowing back to fill the holes in music.

The seventh flares within a lover,
existing only in that moment
when love departs.

The ninth is sometimes glimpsed
after continual gazing

94

at your own reflection in a mirror.

The tenth is a whole world within the bull's-eye,
which archers unknowingly dream at night of striking.

The eleventh is the "point" in space,
as modern physics understands it:
truth or merely tool of thought, but
doesn't really exist.

The twelfth is the fertile quintessence
of desire.

The thirteenth is the fulcrum, pivot of all levers—
the midpoint of every pendulum arc—
the axis of each vortex.

The fourteenth is that insensate moment
preceding and following each sensation.

The fifteenth I saw in the lapsing face
of an old woman on a hospital gurney,
too swollen, too sick, soon to die.

The last is God,
teeming with teeming voids.

SON TO FATHER, RELIGIOUS DISAGREEMENT

Oh, don't chide me
for being naked, don't call me
shameless—

I must be ready
when my Lover comes

INCIDENT ON THE BORDER OF HISTORY

Before we had memory, or language, or a sense of time,
like our brothers and sisters we could not know
what death is—
like rhinoceros, mouse, eagle or trout,
could only blaze in pain and surprise
when its moment exploded within us.

But leaving our purer kin behind,
we came to understand:
Brooded in vague animal fear
till suddenly we could see it
far off, could watch it coming—

And oh this struck at us, at the quick of us—
pierced, in fact, a place within
that had been buried to the point
of not existing at all. But it did.
And when the certain knowledge of death came there,
shaking and fissuring our deepest places,

that dark force became a midwife
bending over our pain,
sweating we cried out, spasmed,
a Child was born, unseen before in this world:

Call it the human spirit

SAYING GRACE AT A NEIGHBOR'S

These aren't frivolous people.

If you toss a ball against a wall, or in the air,
it'll come back to you, happy as a dog—
but these people don't bounce balls
or run beneath an arcing ball to catch it.

If you set words into sentences they'll either
leap together or fall apart—
but these people only say what must be said,
waste nothing for the fire of sounds.

They don't sled or skate or
slide in flat-soled shoes over the packed snow.
They don't jump from the crests of sand dunes
and run downslope in huge strides
where the sand will catch you easily,
jump to jump.

That from this spot, right here,
from this block of tract houses you could travel,
step by step, mile by mile, in any direction,
Angola, Beijing, Patagonia—
this they hardly seem even to consider.

Say prayers for food, the cardboard laws command,
and this they do,
but fidget and mumble through
thy bounty

TIM J. MYERS

TOYS

...because I couldn't find the food I liked. If I had found it, believe me, I should have...stuffed myself like...anyone else.

—Kafka, "The Hunger Artist"

The Hindu concept of "toys"
as Huston Smith describes it:

Let them race to the stores to buy
this season's Barbies and over-stuffed superheroes
for glassy-eyed kids—

Let them access their online accounts,
add to their digital libraries
the latest priceless treasures—

Let them fill their houses with Southwestern bric-a-brac
in pastels utterly foreign to the mesa country—

Let them buy Tesla X's with Falcon Wing doors,
Lamborghinis, Lexus L-C's with Driver-Centric cockpits—

Let them amble from massage table to hot tub
to walk-in closet to home-theater—

Let them cut a dance tune on Ableton,
hit Number 1 and dominate the charts,
make a movie that bangs down
four-hundred mil its opening weekend—

Let them acquire companies foreign and domestic,
string them together like beads;
let them build their Aladdin's-cave portfolios—

Let them.

Someday, someday
(may it come in this life),
someday the sacred animal so deep within the self
will tire at last, will grow
hungry, will know true
hunger, will
long for

food.

WHEN SLEEPY

There's a weariness in us
that lives our lives as we do,
though the beat of drums goes thumping on,
heart sounds out its endless murmurs.
At times we glimpse it;
body's weariness reveals a deeper weariness
we seem to carry as some strange seed in our depths.
We find ourselves thinking
I could close my eyes and sleep
till God breathes on the mud of me
in the next Eden—
this desire as immortal as our selves. I think
all space and time knows the same weariness,
is compounded of it far below
the realm of quarks and probability-clouds.
Sometimes in sleep I open myself to it,
but how astounding—to find
it's somehow a door through which
I step into the deeper clarity of dreams.
It's the weariness of seeds pressed by dark ground,
green husks beginning to split.
It tastes of something far off,
a half-sensed whatever:
something about thick petals whorled tightly together,
their color as of unknown stars,
a fragrance moving through
one kind of life, one universe
into another.

FOR A HYMN TO THE EDGE

out on the reaches of all that is,
on the One sphere's aspherical blurring surface-edges

when time banks up like wind-blown ice on a lake shore

where space eases itself into trailing wisps

when light grows into something else

where thought curls and dwindles like a leaf in utter fire

when reality itself goes shape-shifting away and toward

where geometry melts

when physicality condenses into clouds and rains in
tiny droplets onto
seas of

infinity

Tim J. Myers

HYMN FOR THE EVENTUALITIES

How will it be, how will it be? she said,
when I am gone, flung like so much dust
beyond this body and breath,
still sparkling with the remnant warmth
of what I was?

It will be wandering through all dazzlement,
the sun answered.
Nothing but darkness,
said night.

Body remade, sang chrysalis.
Extinction, ash insisted.

Union with All along the path of lightning!
her soul whispered.
Passion infinite! pounded her heart.

Lapse into unfixed chemicals,
science stated.
Soaring through Om,
the musicians chanted.

Sinking into utter rest,
murmured the weary ones.
Burning endless exultation!
shouted the strong.

Down in the White of the Tree

Oh my life! she cried, and became
like star dies in space, burned to cold stone—
like river at seamouth—
word spoken in air—

was snuffed out, lit up, shaken free, bound tight, danced over,
shattered, lifted, erased,
dead alive reborn extinguished—
finished in a tempest of beginnings.

Then her name

Spoken

FOR MY WIFE

Because I usually live like so many people do,
taking things as they come,
more or less satisfied from day to day,
not asking too much,

but then am jerked upright, suddenly awake,
by the force of my need for her,
by craving am emptied of all that easy comfort,
by yearning suddenly flung out
over a yawning mountain cirque, which is my own desire—

because of this I sometimes feel pity
for those who in their ease and steadiness
sustain themselves, are unafraid, secure,
neither see in themselves blank darkness descending away
nor in that impossible gut-moment
begin, however faintly in terror,

to love the abyss

CREED

Death
slowly
dawns
on
us

TIM J. MYERS

A CHILD'S NIGHT WAKING

From that far darkness
into which the wind of sleep has blown us,
a small cry calls us back.

There's a whiteness to the cry.
For a moment it flickers in us like a first star,
we might confuse it for
the call of a gull out over the water.

But small as it is, it reaches us
across the endless dark prairies of our reveries.

It's our daughter, uneasy in sleep.
She calls again—we're instantly awake,
no longer husband and wife, now only
mother and father.

Something in her cry has burned us;
for an instant it carries all human suffering
and we thrill with fear, because
we love her, hate so deeply
any hurt that might assail her.

We spring from bed,
bare feet cold on the winter floors,
hair mussed with sleep, we can't endure
even the possibility of her pain,

but once in her room see that
it's only a child's night waking.

So one of us will sit beside her
on the bed, stroking her hair
and murmuring the kind of empty words
that mean everything.
The other stands at her bedside for a time,
then perhaps looks out at the moon through her window,
wonders at the luminous midwife moon

who's watched as numberless babies
were born into the world, has
officiated in her way
at these uncountable births,
silent, adorning the whole of things,
doing nothing to help us here but
commanding in some mysterious way,
drawing us on in the business of living,

there in the huge dark above the world
like a single white cry
breaking from
a sleep

TIM J. MYERS

FUNK BAND: A THEOLOGY

(from a passage by Huston Smith)

It was Southside Johnny's on a Friday night,
funk-slash-rock-slash-R&B band
pumping out sex-hot beats in the loud close air,
should've heard the sax guy scat-blowing, snap-growling,
15 unreal choruses to Average White Band's "Pick Up
    the Pieces,"
felt like I might just dance my ass through some sacred
    metaphysical Door—

the body said Plato the body is a tomb

Brick-walled bar with a crowded floor,
everyone up, everyone moving,
the jam too loud but just loud enough,
some kind of crushing luminous presence pouring from
    the amps,
making everything tight, electric, pulse-crazed

body a tomb
the seemingness of forms only Maya illusion most empty

And the chick singing lead, tiny little thing
but she could put it—used that voice
like a big drum, stacking the wild note-lines
till my feet, my lungs, my heart, went tarantella-wild,

109

Down in the White of the Tree

body a tomb   form is empty
Lord Buddha called the world a burning house get out get out

When they started cranking into Junior Walker's "Shotgun,"
everybody knows it, everybody poured onto the floor,
like some spirit tsunami bursting up into us
out of the Earth itself, ground beneath the floor,
I was a song-drunk bird banging skyward, groove so hot

body a tomb   empty forms   burning prison
Jesus said Build no house in this world
Holy Koran insists that
all will be harvested or wither to worthless straw

You sweat buckets when you dance that hard,
comes pouring out all over you, who cares,
the beat the beat the beat the beat,
anoint me in your holy nectar till my clothes are soaked,
during Sly's "Dance to the Music" I started spinning like
    some crazy guy

body a tomb   burning prison   no ground to make one's home
all to be scythed or dead in the field
Master Taishi called the world a lie

God it was sweet! I just kept
riding it riding it, for those few crazed oretic hours
measuring all I am to the bass, its thumping certainty,
felt my boundaries leap laughing away
like guitar solo bird-quick up off the drum-line but always
    returning,
danced and danced, my legs, my chest, my lungs,
oh horn section, horn section, Sufi me! Sufi me!

110

SOMETHING

n orange
crow
white:
know,

question
doubt—
unknowable
out—

olor
ape
verything

111

MILKY WAY

The sky her dark calls out in me
this prayer, my heartwood and sapwood
straining branches toward immaculate night

and toward that jewel-whitened arc across i
small circles set in the glowing dust-bridge–
over which whose feet?
The blessed, the dead.

Invisible and unknown they are walking,
having been uprooted by the stars.
Slow growing but growing wild
they cross over, like small clusters
of fragrant flowers between
some April and some June.

Their deaths coincide
with Death itself,
the wide, sea-risen, star-called movement
of all things.

Those white pastures, those far
and blissful regions of the sky,
upward, outward, and this prayer
forever circling where I stand:
that in my time I too will

go.

112

TIM J. MYERS

Endpiece

MY DEATH SONG

the birds ignore that
edict forbidding joy
in the cemetery

ACKNOWLEDGMENTS

"Grace on a March Morning" first appeared

"Names of God" first appeared in *Color W*

"Junk Windchimes" first appeared in *Wind*

"Before an Ancient Bas-relief" first appeare

"For Edgar Allan Poe" first appeared in *Lit*

"Transphysical Song" first appeared in *Ship*

"After Bernini's Ecstasy of St. Theresa" firs *Christianity and the Arts.*

"Apple Trees in Early Winter" first appeare

"Milky Way" first appeared on the Astropo (Astropoetica.com.)

"For a Hymn to the Edge" first appeared o Astropoetica site (Astropoetica.com.)

"Paleolithic Burial" first appeared in *Santa*